Manners

Manners at a Restaurant

by Terri DeGezelle

Consultant:
Madonna Murphy, PhD, Professor of Education
University of St. Francis, Joliet, Illinois
Author, *Character Education in America's Blue Ribbon Schools*

Capstone *press*

Mankato, Minnesota

First Facts is published by Capstone Press
151 Good Counsel Drive, P.O. Box 669, Mankato, Minnesota 56002
www.capstonepress.com

Library of Congress Cataloging-in-Publication Data
DeGezelle, Terri, 1955–
    Manners at a restaurant / by Terri DeGezelle.
        p. cm.—(First facts. Manners)
    Includes bibliographical references (p. 23) and index.
    ISBN 0-7368-2644-0 (hardcover)
    1. Table etiquette—Juvenile literature. [1. Table etiquette. 2. Etiquette.] I. Title. II. Series.
BJ2041.D44 2005
395.5′4—dc22   2003023368

Summary: Describes good manners and shows how various manners and character values can
    be used when dining at a restaurant.

Editorial Credits
Christine Peterson, editor; Juliette Peters, designer; Wanda Winch, photo researcher; Eric Kudalis,
    product planning editor

Photo Credits
All photos by Capstone Press/Gem Photo Studio/Dan Delaney except page 20,
    Corbis/Lee Snider

Artistic Effects
Capstone Press, 21

1 2 3 4 5 6 09 08 07 06 05 04

Table of Contents

Going to a Restaurant 4

Showing Respect 7

Being Polite 8

Being Patient 10

Considerate Diners 12

Showing Courtesy 14

Keeping Neat 16

Good Manners 18

Amazing but True! 20
Hands On: Table Talk 21
Glossary 22
Read More 23
Internet Sites 23
Index 24

Going to a Restaurant

People can use good **manners** when visiting restaurants. People with good manners are kind and **polite** to others. Everyone enjoys a meal when people use good manners. Chrissy, Ashley, and their grandparents will use good manners at the restaurant.

Fun Fact!
In the United States, there are about 870,000 restaurants.

4

Showing Respect

People can show **respect** when being seated. People show respect when they think of others. The greeter shows the family to a table. Ashley, Chrissy, and their grandparents talk quietly so they do not bother other people.

> **Fun Fact!**
> More people eat out on Saturday than any other day of the week.

Being Polite

Polite people wait to sit down until everyone is at the table. **Diners** place napkins on their laps. They sit up straight in their chairs.

Diners read the menu and choose what they want to eat. Polite diners take turns ordering. They speak clearly and say "thank you" to the server.

Being Patient

Diners use good manners when they are **patient**. Diners are patient as they wait for their food to arrive. They wait quietly without complaining. They wait to eat until everyone is served. The family then enjoys a meal together.

Fun Fact!
In the United States, people order fried chicken more than any other food.

Considerate Diners

Considerate diners care about others when eating. They use good manners. They take small bites of food. They chew with their mouths closed.

Ashley and her grandmother talk during the meal. Considerate people listen without **interrupting**. They also finish chewing before talking.

Showing Courtesy

People can show **courtesy** when dining. They can ask others nicely to pass food. They keep their elbows off the table.

People show courtesy when they need more to drink. People say "please" when they ask for more milk. They say "thank you" when it arrives.

Keeping Neat

Diners keep neat when eating their
meals. Ashley keeps neat by wiping her
mouth with a napkin. She keeps her
sleeves out of the food.

Diners sometimes spill drinks or food on the table. Chrissy asks the server to help. She wipes up the spill. Chrissy thanks the server for her help.

Good Manners

Ashley, Chrissy, and their grandparents share a big dessert. The family uses good manners. They are polite to the server and each other. Everyone enjoys going to a restaurant when people use good manners.

Amazing but True!

The White Horse Tavern in Rhode Island is the oldest U.S. restaurant. The building was put up in 1673. In 1687, it opened as a restaurant. Some leaders of the 13 Colonies ate there. People still eat at the restaurant today.

Hands On: Table Talk

People use good manners when they talk politely with others at a restaurant. Play this game to practice talking politely with friends.

What You Need

friends
table
small beanbag

What You Do

1. Invite all the players to sit around a table.
2. One player starts by asking a question. That player then gently slides the beanbag to someone sitting at the table.
3. The person who gets the beanbag says "thank you." The second player then answers the question. Other players may not speak until they get the beanbag.
4. The second player asks another question. He or she then slides the beanbag to someone else at the table.
5. Players slide the beanbag back and forth around the table until everyone has asked and answered a question.

Glossary

considerate (kuhn-SID-uh-rit)—thoughtful of the needs and feelings of other people

courtesy (KUR-tuh-see)—behaving in a way that shows good behavior toward others

diner (DYE-nur)—a person eating in a restaurant

interrupt (in-tuh-RUHPT)—to begin talking before someone has finished speaking

manners (MAN-urss)—polite behavior

patient (PAY–shuhnt)—able to wait quietly without getting angry or upset

polite (puh-LITE)—to have good manners; polite people are kind and thoughtful.

respect (ri-SPEKT)—belief in the quality and worth of others, yourself, and your surroundings

Read More

Doudna, Kelly. *Excuse Me.* Good Manners. Edina, Minn.: Abdo, 2001.

Raatma, Lucia. *Politeness.* Character Education. Mankato, Minn.: Bridgestone Books, 2002.

Internet Sites

FactHound offers a safe, fun way to find Internet sites related to this book. All of the sites on FactHound have been researched by our staff.

Here's how:
1. Visit *www.facthound.com*
2. Type in this special code **0736826440** for age-appropriate sites. Or enter a search word related to this book for a more general search.
3. Click on **Fetch It** button.

FactHound will fetch the best sites for you!

Index

chairs, 8
considerate, 12–13
courtesy, 14–15

dessert, 18
diners, 8, 9, 10, 12, 16, 17

eating, 7, 9, 10, 12, 16, 20
elbows, 14

food, 10, 12, 14, 16, 17

greeter, 7

interrupt, 13

listen, 13

meals, 4, 10, 13, 16
menus, 9
milk, 15

napkins, 8, 16
neat, 16–17

order, 9, 10

patient, 10
please, 15
polite, 4, 8–9, 18

respect, 7

servers, 9, 17, 18
spill, 17

tables, 7, 8, 14, 17
taking turns, 9
thank you, 9, 15

wait, 8, 10
White Horse Tavern, 20